PUBLISHED BY SPENCE & CO.

DISCLAIMER:

THE CONTENT OF THIS JOURNAL IS INTENDED FOR PERSONAL REFLECTION AND SUPPORT. IT IS NOT A SUBSTITUTE FOR PROFESSIONAL MEDICAL, PSYCHOLOGICAL, FINANCIAL, OR LEGAL ADVICE. READERS SHOULD CONSULT QUALIFIED PROFESSIONALS AS NEEDED.

Some seasons ask more from us than we have to give.

This journal exists for those seasons.

It is a place to pause, to think clearly, and to steady yourself when life feels uncertain or heavy. You won't find forced positivity here, or pressure to feel grateful when you're exhausted.

You may come to these pages frustrated, overwhelmed, numb, or unsure. All of that belongs.

Use this journal as a quiet support. A place to organise your thoughts, tend to what matters most, and let the rest wait.

Return as often or as rarely as you need.

— Spence & Co.

DATE: / /

Grounding Page

WHAT FEELS MOST URGENT RIGHT NOW?

WHAT CAN BE ADDRESSED TODAY WITHOUT OVERLOAD?

WHAT CAN SAFELY WAIT?

ONE SMALL ACTION TO REGAIN CLARITY:

DATE: / /

Capacity Check!

HOW MUCH ENERGY DO I REALISTICALLY HAVE TODAY?

WHERE AM I OVEREXTENDING?

WHAT CAN BE SIMPLIFIED, POSTPONED, OR DROPPED?

ONE ADJUSTMENT TO MAKE TODAY MANAGEABLE:

DATE: / /

Hard Truth/Kind Response

HARD TRUTH: THE REALITY I AM FACING?

HARD TRUTH: WHAT WORRIES ME THE MOST?

KIND RESPONSE: WHAT I ACTUALLY KNOW?

KIND RESPONSE: WHAT IS WITHIN MY CONTROL?

DATE: / /

Support Inventory

WHO OR WHAT HAS HELPED ME RECENTLY?

WHERE AM I CARRYING TOO MUCH ALONE?

ONE FORM OF SUPPORT I COULD ACCEPT OR SEEK?

DATE: / /

Financial & Life Stress

CURRENT FINANCIAL STRESSOR?

WHAT IS OUTSIDE OF MY CONTROL?

WHAT IS REALISTICALLY MANAGEABLE THIS WEEK?

ONE STABILISING STEP I CAN TAKE:

DATE: / /

Steadying Reflection

WHAT SMALL ACTION HELPED TODAY?

WHAT WILL I CONTINUE?

WHAT CAN I RELEASE FOR NOW?

WHAT FEELS MORE STABLE THAN BEFORE?

DATE: / /

Grounding Page

WHAT FEELS MOST URGENT RIGHT NOW?

WHAT CAN BE ADDRESSED TODAY WITHOUT OVERLOAD?

WHAT CAN SAFELY WAIT?

ONE SMALL ACTION TO REGAIN CLARITY:

DATE: / /

Capacity Check!

HOW MUCH ENERGY DO I REALISTICALLY HAVE TODAY?

WHERE AM I OVEREXTENDING?

WHAT CAN BE SIMPLIFIED, POSTPONED, OR DROPPED?

ONE ADJUSTMENT TO MAKE TODAY MANAGEABLE:

DATE: / /

Hard Truth/Kind Response

HARD TRUTH: THE REALITY I AM FACING?

HARD TRUTH: WHAT WORRIES ME THE MOST?

KIND RESPONSE: WHAT I ACTUALLY KNOW?

KIND RESPONSE: WHAT IS WITHIN MY CONTROL?

DATE: / /

Support Inventory

WHO OR WHAT HAS HELPED ME RECENTLY?

WHERE AM I CARRYING TOO MUCH ALONE?

ONE FORM OF SUPPORT I COULD ACCEPT OR SEEK?

DATE: / /

Financial & Life Stress

CURRENT FINANCIAL STRESSOR?

WHAT IS OUTSIDE OF MY CONTROL?

WHAT IS REALISTICALLY MANAGEABLE THIS WEEK?

ONE STABILISING STEP I CAN TAKE:

DATE: / /

Steadying Reflection

WHAT SMALL ACTION HELPED TODAY?

WHAT WILL I CONTINUE?

WHAT CAN I RELEASE FOR NOW?

WHAT FEELS MORE STABLE THAN BEFORE?

DATE: / /

Grounding Page

WHAT FEELS MOST URGENT RIGHT NOW?

WHAT CAN BE ADDRESSED TODAY WITHOUT OVERLOAD?

WHAT CAN SAFELY WAIT?

ONE SMALL ACTION TO REGAIN CLARITY:

DATE: / /

Capacity Check!

HOW MUCH ENERGY DO I REALISTICALLY HAVE TODAY?

WHERE AM I OVEREXTENDING?

WHAT CAN BE SIMPLIFIED, POSTPONED, OR DROPPED?

ONE ADJUSTMENT TO MAKE TODAY MANAGEABLE:

DATE: / /

Hard Truth/Kind Response

HARD TRUTH: THE REALITY I AM FACING?

HARD TRUTH: WHAT WORRIES ME THE MOST?

KIND RESPONSE: WHAT I ACTUALLY KNOW?

KIND RESPONSE: WHAT IS WITHIN MY CONTROL?

DATE: / /

Support Inventory

WHO OR WHAT HAS HELPED ME RECENTLY?

WHERE AM I CARRYING TOO MUCH ALONE?

ONE FORM OF SUPPORT I COULD ACCEPT OR SEEK?

DATE: / /

Financial & Life Stress

CURRENT FINANCIAL STRESSOR?

WHAT IS OUTSIDE OF MY CONTROL?

WHAT IS REALISTICALLY MANAGEABLE THIS WEEK?

ONE STABILISING STEP I CAN TAKE:

DATE: / /

Steadying Reflection

WHAT SMALL ACTION HELPED TODAY?

WHAT WILL I CONTINUE?

WHAT CAN I RELEASE FOR NOW?

WHAT FEELS MORE STABLE THAN BEFORE?

DATE: / /

Grounding Page

WHAT FEELS MOST URGENT RIGHT NOW?

WHAT CAN BE ADDRESSED TODAY WITHOUT OVERLOAD?

WHAT CAN SAFELY WAIT?

ONE SMALL ACTION TO REGAIN CLARITY:

DATE: / /

Capacity Check!

HOW MUCH ENERGY DO I REALISTICALLY HAVE TODAY?

WHERE AM I OVEREXTENDING?

WHAT CAN BE SIMPLIFIED, POSTPONED, OR DROPPED?

ONE ADJUSTMENT TO MAKE TODAY MANAGEABLE:

DATE: / /

Hard Truth/Kind Response

HARD TRUTH: THE REALITY I AM FACING?

HARD TRUTH: WHAT WORRIES ME THE MOST?

KIND RESPONSE: WHAT I ACTUALLY KNOW?

KIND RESPONSE: WHAT IS WITHIN MY CONTROL?

DATE: / /

Support Inventory

WHO OR WHAT HAS HELPED ME RECENTLY?

WHERE AM I CARRYING TOO MUCH ALONE?

ONE FORM OF SUPPORT I COULD ACCEPT OR SEEK?

DATE: / /

Financial & Life Stress

CURRENT FINANCIAL STRESSOR?

WHAT IS OUTSIDE OF MY CONTROL?

WHAT IS REALISTICALLY MANAGEABLE THIS WEEK?

ONE STABILISING STEP I CAN TAKE:

DATE: / /

Steadying Reflection

WHAT SMALL ACTION HELPED TODAY?

WHAT WILL I CONTINUE?

WHAT CAN I RELEASE FOR NOW?

WHAT FEELS MORE STABLE THAN BEFORE?

DATE: / /

Grounding Page

WHAT FEELS MOST URGENT RIGHT NOW?

WHAT CAN BE ADDRESSED TODAY WITHOUT OVERLOAD?

WHAT CAN SAFELY WAIT?

ONE SMALL ACTION TO REGAIN CLARITY:

DATE: / /

Capacity Check!

HOW MUCH ENERGY DO I REALISTICALLY HAVE TODAY?

WHERE AM I OVEREXTENDING?

WHAT CAN BE SIMPLIFIED, POSTPONED, OR DROPPED?

ONE ADJUSTMENT TO MAKE TODAY MANAGEABLE:

DATE: / /

Hard Truth/Kind Response

HARD TRUTH: THE REALITY I AM FACING?

HARD TRUTH: WHAT WORRIES ME THE MOST?

KIND RESPONSE: WHAT I ACTUALLY KNOW?

KIND RESPONSE: WHAT IS WITHIN MY CONTROL?

DATE: / /

Support Inventory

WHO OR WHAT HAS HELPED ME RECENTLY?

WHERE AM I CARRYING TOO MUCH ALONE?

ONE FORM OF SUPPORT I COULD ACCEPT OR SEEK?

DATE: / /

Financial & Life Stress

CURRENT FINANCIAL STRESSOR?

WHAT IS OUTSIDE OF MY CONTROL?

WHAT IS REALISTICALLY MANAGEABLE THIS WEEK?

ONE STABILISING STEP I CAN TAKE:

DATE: / /

Steadying Reflection

WHAT SMALL ACTION HELPED TODAY?

WHAT WILL I CONTINUE?

WHAT CAN I RELEASE FOR NOW?

WHAT FEELS MORE STABLE THAN BEFORE?

DATE: / /

Grounding Page

WHAT FEELS MOST URGENT RIGHT NOW?

WHAT CAN BE ADDRESSED TODAY WITHOUT OVERLOAD?

WHAT CAN SAFELY WAIT?

ONE SMALL ACTION TO REGAIN CLARITY:

DATE: / /

Capacity Check!

HOW MUCH ENERGY DO I REALISTICALLY HAVE TODAY?

WHERE AM I OVEREXTENDING?

WHAT CAN BE SIMPLIFIED, POSTPONED, OR DROPPED?

ONE ADJUSTMENT TO MAKE TODAY MANAGEABLE:

DATE: / /

Hard Truth/Kind Response

HARD TRUTH: THE REALITY I AM FACING?

HARD TRUTH: WHAT WORRIES ME THE MOST?

KIND RESPONSE: WHAT I ACTUALLY KNOW?

KIND RESPONSE: WHAT IS WITHIN MY CONTROL?

DATE: / /

Support Inventory

WHO OR WHAT HAS HELPED ME RECENTLY?

WHERE AM I CARRYING TOO MUCH ALONE?

ONE FORM OF SUPPORT I COULD ACCEPT OR SEEK?

DATE: / /

Financial & Life Stress

CURRENT FINANCIAL STRESSOR?

WHAT IS OUTSIDE OF MY CONTROL?

WHAT IS REALISTICALLY MANAGEABLE THIS WEEK?

ONE STABILISING STEP I CAN TAKE:

DATE: / /

Steadying Reflection

WHAT SMALL ACTION HELPED TODAY?

WHAT WILL I CONTINUE?

WHAT CAN I RELEASE FOR NOW?

WHAT FEELS MORE STABLE THAN BEFORE?

DATE: / /

Grounding Page

WHAT FEELS MOST URGENT RIGHT NOW?

WHAT CAN BE ADDRESSED TODAY WITHOUT OVERLOAD?

WHAT CAN SAFELY WAIT?

ONE SMALL ACTION TO REGAIN CLARITY:

DATE: / /

Capacity Check!

HOW MUCH ENERGY DO I REALISTICALLY HAVE TODAY?

WHERE AM I OVEREXTENDING?

WHAT CAN BE SIMPLIFIED, POSTPONED, OR DROPPED?

ONE ADJUSTMENT TO MAKE TODAY MANAGEABLE:

DATE: / /

Hard Truth/Kind Response

HARD TRUTH: THE REALITY I AM FACING?

HARD TRUTH: WHAT WORRIES ME THE MOST?

KIND RESPONSE: WHAT I ACTUALLY KNOW?

KIND RESPONSE: WHAT IS WITHIN MY CONTROL?

DATE: / /

Support Inventory

WHO OR WHAT HAS HELPED ME RECENTLY?

WHERE AM I CARRYING TOO MUCH ALONE?

ONE FORM OF SUPPORT I COULD ACCEPT OR SEEK?

DATE: / /

Financial & Life Stress

CURRENT FINANCIAL STRESSOR?

WHAT IS OUTSIDE OF MY CONTROL?

WHAT IS REALISTICALLY MANAGEABLE THIS WEEK?

ONE STABILISING STEP I CAN TAKE:

DATE: / /

Steadying Reflection

WHAT SMALL ACTION HELPED TODAY?

WHAT WILL I CONTINUE?

WHAT CAN I RELEASE FOR NOW?

WHAT FEELS MORE STABLE THAN BEFORE?

DATE: / /

Grounding Page

WHAT FEELS MOST URGENT RIGHT NOW?

WHAT CAN BE ADDRESSED TODAY WITHOUT OVERLOAD?

WHAT CAN SAFELY WAIT?

ONE SMALL ACTION TO REGAIN CLARITY:

DATE: / /

Capacity Check!

HOW MUCH ENERGY DO I REALISTICALLY HAVE TODAY?

WHERE AM I OVEREXTENDING?

WHAT CAN BE SIMPLIFIED, POSTPONED, OR DROPPED?

ONE ADJUSTMENT TO MAKE TODAY MANAGEABLE:

DATE: / /

Hard Truth/Kind Response

HARD TRUTH: THE REALITY I AM FACING?

HARD TRUTH: WHAT WORRIES ME THE MOST?

KIND RESPONSE: WHAT I ACTUALLY KNOW?

KIND RESPONSE: WHAT IS WITHIN MY CONTROL?

DATE: / /

Support Inventory

WHO OR WHAT HAS HELPED ME RECENTLY?

WHERE AM I CARRYING TOO MUCH ALONE?

ONE FORM OF SUPPORT I COULD ACCEPT OR SEEK?

DATE: / /

Financial & Life Stress

CURRENT FINANCIAL STRESSOR?

WHAT IS OUTSIDE OF MY CONTROL?

WHAT IS REALISTICALLY MANAGEABLE THIS WEEK?

ONE STABILISING STEP I CAN TAKE:

DATE: / /

Steadying Reflection

WHAT SMALL ACTION HELPED TODAY?

WHAT WILL I CONTINUE?

WHAT CAN I RELEASE FOR NOW?

WHAT FEELS MORE STABLE THAN BEFORE?

DATE: / /

Grounding Page

WHAT FEELS MOST URGENT RIGHT NOW?

WHAT CAN BE ADDRESSED TODAY WITHOUT OVERLOAD?

WHAT CAN SAFELY WAIT?

ONE SMALL ACTION TO REGAIN CLARITY:

DATE: / /

Capacity Check!

HOW MUCH ENERGY DO I REALISTICALLY HAVE TODAY?

WHERE AM I OVEREXTENDING?

WHAT CAN BE SIMPLIFIED, POSTPONED, OR DROPPED?

ONE ADJUSTMENT TO MAKE TODAY MANAGEABLE:

DATE: / /

Hard Truth/Kind Response

HARD TRUTH: THE REALITY I AM FACING?

HARD TRUTH: WHAT WORRIES ME THE MOST?

KIND RESPONSE: WHAT I ACTUALLY KNOW?

KIND RESPONSE: WHAT IS WITHIN MY CONTROL?

DATE: / /

Support Inventory

WHO OR WHAT HAS HELPED ME RECENTLY?

WHERE AM I CARRYING TOO MUCH ALONE?

ONE FORM OF SUPPORT I COULD ACCEPT OR SEEK?

DATE: / /

Financial & Life Stress

CURRENT FINANCIAL STRESSOR?

WHAT IS OUTSIDE OF MY CONTROL?

WHAT IS REALISTICALLY MANAGEABLE THIS WEEK?

ONE STABILISING STEP I CAN TAKE:

DATE: / /

Steadying Reflection

WHAT SMALL ACTION HELPED TODAY?

WHAT WILL I CONTINUE?

WHAT CAN I RELEASE FOR NOW?

WHAT FEELS MORE STABLE THAN BEFORE?

DATE: / /

Grounding Page

WHAT FEELS MOST URGENT RIGHT NOW?

WHAT CAN BE ADDRESSED TODAY WITHOUT OVERLOAD?

WHAT CAN SAFELY WAIT?

ONE SMALL ACTION TO REGAIN CLARITY:

DATE: / /

Capacity Check!

HOW MUCH ENERGY DO I REALISTICALLY HAVE TODAY?

WHERE AM I OVEREXTENDING?

WHAT CAN BE SIMPLIFIED, POSTPONED, OR DROPPED?

ONE ADJUSTMENT TO MAKE TODAY MANAGEABLE:

DATE: / /

Hard Truth/Kind Response

HARD TRUTH: THE REALITY I AM FACING?

HARD TRUTH: WHAT WORRIES ME THE MOST?

KIND RESPONSE: WHAT I ACTUALLY KNOW?

KIND RESPONSE: WHAT IS WITHIN MY CONTROL?

DATE: / /

Support Inventory

WHO OR WHAT HAS HELPED ME RECENTLY?

WHERE AM I CARRYING TOO MUCH ALONE?

ONE FORM OF SUPPORT I COULD ACCEPT OR SEEK?

DATE: / /

Financial & Life Stress

CURRENT FINANCIAL STRESSOR?

WHAT IS OUTSIDE OF MY CONTROL?

WHAT IS REALISTICALLY MANAGEABLE THIS WEEK?

ONE STABILISING STEP I CAN TAKE:

DATE: / /

Steadying Reflection

WHAT SMALL ACTION HELPED TODAY?

WHAT WILL I CONTINUE?

WHAT CAN I RELEASE FOR NOW?

WHAT FEELS MORE STABLE THAN BEFORE?

DATE: / /

Grounding Page

WHAT FEELS MOST URGENT RIGHT NOW?

WHAT CAN BE ADDRESSED TODAY WITHOUT OVERLOAD?

WHAT CAN SAFELY WAIT?

ONE SMALL ACTION TO REGAIN CLARITY:

DATE: / /

Capacity Check!

HOW MUCH ENERGY DO I REALISTICALLY HAVE TODAY?

WHERE AM I OVEREXTENDING?

WHAT CAN BE SIMPLIFIED, POSTPONED, OR DROPPED?

ONE ADJUSTMENT TO MAKE TODAY MANAGEABLE:

DATE: / /

Hard Truth/Kind Response

HARD TRUTH: THE REALITY I AM FACING?

HARD TRUTH: WHAT WORRIES ME THE MOST?

KIND RESPONSE: WHAT I ACTUALLY KNOW?

KIND RESPONSE: WHAT IS WITHIN MY CONTROL?

DATE: / /

Support Inventory

WHO OR WHAT HAS HELPED ME RECENTLY?

WHERE AM I CARRYING TOO MUCH ALONE?

ONE FORM OF SUPPORT I COULD ACCEPT OR SEEK?

DATE: / /

Financial & Life Stress

CURRENT FINANCIAL STRESSOR?

WHAT IS OUTSIDE OF MY CONTROL?

WHAT IS REALISTICALLY MANAGEABLE THIS WEEK?

ONE STABILISING STEP I CAN TAKE:

DATE: / /

Steadying Reflection

WHAT SMALL ACTION HELPED TODAY?

WHAT WILL I CONTINUE?

WHAT CAN I RELEASE FOR NOW?

WHAT FEELS MORE STABLE THAN BEFORE?

DATE: / /

Grounding Page

WHAT FEELS MOST URGENT RIGHT NOW?

WHAT CAN BE ADDRESSED TODAY WITHOUT OVERLOAD?

WHAT CAN SAFELY WAIT?

ONE SMALL ACTION TO REGAIN CLARITY:

DATE: / /

Capacity Check!

HOW MUCH ENERGY DO I REALISTICALLY HAVE TODAY?

WHERE AM I OVEREXTENDING?

WHAT CAN BE SIMPLIFIED, POSTPONED, OR DROPPED?

ONE ADJUSTMENT TO MAKE TODAY MANAGEABLE:

DATE: / /

Hard Truth/Kind Response

HARD TRUTH: THE REALITY I AM FACING?

HARD TRUTH: WHAT WORRIES ME THE MOST?

KIND RESPONSE: WHAT I ACTUALLY KNOW?

KIND RESPONSE: WHAT IS WITHIN MY CONTROL?

DATE: / /

Support Inventory

WHO OR WHAT HAS HELPED ME RECENTLY?

WHERE AM I CARRYING TOO MUCH ALONE?

ONE FORM OF SUPPORT I COULD ACCEPT OR SEEK?

DATE: / /

Financial & Life Stress

CURRENT FINANCIAL STRESSOR?

WHAT IS OUTSIDE OF MY CONTROL?

WHAT IS REALISTICALLY MANAGEABLE THIS WEEK?

ONE STABILISING STEP I CAN TAKE:

DATE: / /

Steadying Reflection

WHAT SMALL ACTION HELPED TODAY?

WHAT WILL I CONTINUE?

WHAT CAN I RELEASE FOR NOW?

WHAT FEELS MORE STABLE THAN BEFORE?

DATE: / /

Grounding Page

WHAT FEELS MOST URGENT RIGHT NOW?

WHAT CAN BE ADDRESSED TODAY WITHOUT OVERLOAD?

WHAT CAN SAFELY WAIT?

ONE SMALL ACTION TO REGAIN CLARITY:

DATE: / /

Capacity Check!

HOW MUCH ENERGY DO I REALISTICALLY HAVE TODAY?

WHERE AM I OVEREXTENDING?

WHAT CAN BE SIMPLIFIED, POSTPONED, OR DROPPED?

ONE ADJUSTMENT TO MAKE TODAY MANAGEABLE:

DATE: / /

Hard Truth/Kind Response

HARD TRUTH: THE REALITY I AM FACING?

HARD TRUTH: WHAT WORRIES ME THE MOST?

KIND RESPONSE: WHAT I ACTUALLY KNOW?

KIND RESPONSE: WHAT IS WITHIN MY CONTROL?

DATE: / /

Support Inventory

WHO OR WHAT HAS HELPED ME RECENTLY?

WHERE AM I CARRYING TOO MUCH ALONE?

ONE FORM OF SUPPORT I COULD ACCEPT OR SEEK?

DATE: / /

Financial & Life Stress

CURRENT FINANCIAL STRESSOR?

WHAT IS OUTSIDE OF MY CONTROL?

WHAT IS REALISTICALLY MANAGEABLE THIS WEEK?

ONE STABILISING STEP I CAN TAKE:

DATE: / /

Steadying Reflection

WHAT SMALL ACTION HELPED TODAY?

WHAT WILL I CONTINUE?

WHAT CAN I RELEASE FOR NOW?

WHAT FEELS MORE STABLE THAN BEFORE?

DATE: / /

Grounding Page

WHAT FEELS MOST URGENT RIGHT NOW?

WHAT CAN BE ADDRESSED TODAY WITHOUT OVERLOAD?

WHAT CAN SAFELY WAIT?

ONE SMALL ACTION TO REGAIN CLARITY:

DATE: / /

Capacity Check!

HOW MUCH ENERGY DO I REALISTICALLY HAVE TODAY?

WHERE AM I OVEREXTENDING?

WHAT CAN BE SIMPLIFIED, POSTPONED, OR DROPPED?

ONE ADJUSTMENT TO MAKE TODAY MANAGEABLE:

DATE: / /

Hard Truth/Kind Response

HARD TRUTH: THE REALITY I AM FACING?

HARD TRUTH: WHAT WORRIES ME THE MOST?

KIND RESPONSE: WHAT I ACTUALLY KNOW?

KIND RESPONSE: WHAT IS WITHIN MY CONTROL?

DATE: / /

Support Inventory

WHO OR WHAT HAS HELPED ME RECENTLY?

WHERE AM I CARRYING TOO MUCH ALONE?

ONE FORM OF SUPPORT I COULD ACCEPT OR SEEK?

DATE: / /

Financial & Life Stress

CURRENT FINANCIAL STRESSOR?

WHAT IS OUTSIDE OF MY CONTROL?

WHAT IS REALISTICALLY MANAGEABLE THIS WEEK?

ONE STABILISING STEP I CAN TAKE:

DATE: / /

Steadying Reflection

WHAT SMALL ACTION HELPED TODAY?

WHAT WILL I CONTINUE?

WHAT CAN I RELEASE FOR NOW?

WHAT FEELS MORE STABLE THAN BEFORE?

Grounding Page

DATE: / /

WHAT FEELS MOST URGENT RIGHT NOW?

WHAT CAN BE ADDRESSED TODAY WITHOUT OVERLOAD?

WHAT CAN SAFELY WAIT?

ONE SMALL ACTION TO REGAIN CLARITY:

DATE: / /

Capacity Check!

HOW MUCH ENERGY DO I REALISTICALLY HAVE TODAY?

WHERE AM I OVEREXTENDING?

WHAT CAN BE SIMPLIFIED, POSTPONED, OR DROPPED?

ONE ADJUSTMENT TO MAKE TODAY MANAGEABLE:

DATE: / /

Hard Truth/Kind Response

HARD TRUTH: THE REALITY I AM FACING?

HARD TRUTH: WHAT WORRIES ME THE MOST?

KIND RESPONSE: WHAT I ACTUALLY KNOW?

KIND RESPONSE: WHAT IS WITHIN MY CONTROL?

DATE: / /

Support Inventory

WHO OR WHAT HAS HELPED ME RECENTLY?

WHERE AM I CARRYING TOO MUCH ALONE?

ONE FORM OF SUPPORT I COULD ACCEPT OR SEEK?

DATE: / /

Financial & Life Stress

CURRENT FINANCIAL STRESSOR?

WHAT IS OUTSIDE OF MY CONTROL?

WHAT IS REALISTICALLY MANAGEABLE THIS WEEK?

ONE STABILISING STEP I CAN TAKE:

DATE: / /

Steadying Reflection

WHAT SMALL ACTION HELPED TODAY?

WHAT WILL I CONTINUE?

WHAT CAN I RELEASE FOR NOW?

WHAT FEELS MORE STABLE THAN BEFORE?

Grounding Page

DATE: / /

WHAT FEELS MOST URGENT RIGHT NOW?

WHAT CAN BE ADDRESSED TODAY WITHOUT OVERLOAD?

WHAT CAN SAFELY WAIT?

ONE SMALL ACTION TO REGAIN CLARITY:

DATE: / /

Capacity Check!

HOW MUCH ENERGY DO I REALISTICALLY HAVE TODAY?

WHERE AM I OVEREXTENDING?

WHAT CAN BE SIMPLIFIED, POSTPONED, OR DROPPED?

ONE ADJUSTMENT TO MAKE TODAY MANAGEABLE:

DATE: / /

Hard Truth/Kind Response

HARD TRUTH: THE REALITY I AM FACING?

HARD TRUTH: WHAT WORRIES ME THE MOST?

KIND RESPONSE: WHAT I ACTUALLY KNOW?

KIND RESPONSE: WHAT IS WITHIN MY CONTROL?

DATE: / /

Support Inventory

WHO OR WHAT HAS HELPED ME RECENTLY?

WHERE AM I CARRYING TOO MUCH ALONE?

ONE FORM OF SUPPORT I COULD ACCEPT OR SEEK?

DATE: / /

Financial & Life Stress

CURRENT FINANCIAL STRESSOR?

WHAT IS OUTSIDE OF MY CONTROL?

WHAT IS REALISTICALLY MANAGEABLE THIS WEEK?

ONE STABILISING STEP I CAN TAKE:

DATE: / /

Steadying Reflection

WHAT SMALL ACTION HELPED TODAY?

WHAT WILL I CONTINUE?

WHAT CAN I RELEASE FOR NOW?

WHAT FEELS MORE STABLE THAN BEFORE?

DATE: / /

Grounding Page

WHAT FEELS MOST URGENT RIGHT NOW?

WHAT CAN BE ADDRESSED TODAY WITHOUT OVERLOAD?

WHAT CAN SAFELY WAIT?

ONE SMALL ACTION TO REGAIN CLARITY:

DATE: / /

Capacity Check!

HOW MUCH ENERGY DO I REALISTICALLY HAVE TODAY?

WHERE AM I OVEREXTENDING?

WHAT CAN BE SIMPLIFIED, POSTPONED, OR DROPPED?

ONE ADJUSTMENT TO MAKE TODAY MANAGEABLE:

DATE: / /

Hard Truth/Kind Response

HARD TRUTH: THE REALITY I AM FACING?

HARD TRUTH: WHAT WORRIES ME THE MOST?

KIND RESPONSE: WHAT I ACTUALLY KNOW?

KIND RESPONSE: WHAT IS WITHIN MY CONTROL?

DATE: / /

Support Inventory

WHO OR WHAT HAS HELPED ME RECENTLY?

WHERE AM I CARRYING TOO MUCH ALONE?

ONE FORM OF SUPPORT I COULD ACCEPT OR SEEK?

DATE: / /

Financial & Life Stress

CURRENT FINANCIAL STRESSOR?

WHAT IS OUTSIDE OF MY CONTROL?

WHAT IS REALISTICALLY MANAGEABLE THIS WEEK?

ONE STABILISING STEP I CAN TAKE:

DATE: / /

Steadying Reflection

WHAT SMALL ACTION HELPED TODAY?

WHAT WILL I CONTINUE?

WHAT CAN I RELEASE FOR NOW?

WHAT FEELS MORE STABLE THAN BEFORE?

DATE: / /

Grounding Page

WHAT FEELS MOST URGENT RIGHT NOW?

WHAT CAN BE ADDRESSED TODAY WITHOUT OVERLOAD?

WHAT CAN SAFELY WAIT?

ONE SMALL ACTION TO REGAIN CLARITY:

DATE: / /

Capacity Check!

HOW MUCH ENERGY DO I REALISTICALLY HAVE TODAY?

WHERE AM I OVEREXTENDING?

WHAT CAN BE SIMPLIFIED, POSTPONED, OR DROPPED?

ONE ADJUSTMENT TO MAKE TODAY MANAGEABLE:

DATE: / /

Hard Truth/Kind Response

HARD TRUTH: THE REALITY I AM FACING?

HARD TRUTH: WHAT WORRIES ME THE MOST?

KIND RESPONSE: WHAT I ACTUALLY KNOW?

KIND RESPONSE: WHAT IS WITHIN MY CONTROL?

DATE: / /

Support Inventory

WHO OR WHAT HAS HELPED ME RECENTLY?

WHERE AM I CARRYING TOO MUCH ALONE?

ONE FORM OF SUPPORT I COULD ACCEPT OR SEEK?

DATE: / /

Financial & Life Stress

CURRENT FINANCIAL STRESSOR?

WHAT IS OUTSIDE OF MY CONTROL?

WHAT IS REALISTICALLY MANAGEABLE THIS WEEK?

ONE STABILISING STEP I CAN TAKE:

DATE: / /

Steadying Reflection

WHAT SMALL ACTION HELPED TODAY?

WHAT WILL I CONTINUE?

WHAT CAN I RELEASE FOR NOW?

WHAT FEELS MORE STABLE THAN BEFORE?

DATE: / /

Grounding Page

WHAT FEELS MOST URGENT RIGHT NOW?

WHAT CAN BE ADDRESSED TODAY WITHOUT OVERLOAD?

WHAT CAN SAFELY WAIT?

ONE SMALL ACTION TO REGAIN CLARITY:

DATE: / /

Capacity Check!

HOW MUCH ENERGY DO I REALISTICALLY HAVE TODAY?

WHERE AM I OVEREXTENDING?

WHAT CAN BE SIMPLIFIED, POSTPONED, OR DROPPED?

ONE ADJUSTMENT TO MAKE TODAY MANAGEABLE:

DATE: / /

Hard Truth/Kind Response

HARD TRUTH: THE REALITY I AM FACING?

HARD TRUTH: WHAT WORRIES ME THE MOST?

KIND RESPONSE: WHAT I ACTUALLY KNOW?

KIND RESPONSE: WHAT IS WITHIN MY CONTROL?

DATE: / /

Support Inventory

WHO OR WHAT HAS HELPED ME RECENTLY?

WHERE AM I CARRYING TOO MUCH ALONE?

ONE FORM OF SUPPORT I COULD ACCEPT OR SEEK?

DATE: / /

Financial & Life Stress

CURRENT FINANCIAL STRESSOR?

WHAT IS OUTSIDE OF MY CONTROL?

WHAT IS REALISTICALLY MANAGEABLE THIS WEEK?

ONE STABILISING STEP I CAN TAKE:

DATE: / /

Steadying Reflection

WHAT SMALL ACTION HELPED TODAY?

WHAT WILL I CONTINUE?

WHAT CAN I RELEASE FOR NOW?

WHAT FEELS MORE STABLE THAN BEFORE?

DATE: / /

Grounding Page

WHAT FEELS MOST URGENT RIGHT NOW?

WHAT CAN BE ADDRESSED TODAY WITHOUT OVERLOAD?

WHAT CAN SAFELY WAIT?

ONE SMALL ACTION TO REGAIN CLARITY:

DATE: / /

Capacity Check!

HOW MUCH ENERGY DO I REALISTICALLY HAVE TODAY?

WHERE AM I OVEREXTENDING?

WHAT CAN BE SIMPLIFIED, POSTPONED, OR DROPPED?

ONE ADJUSTMENT TO MAKE TODAY MANAGEABLE:

DATE: / /

Hard Truth/Kind Response

HARD TRUTH: THE REALITY I AM FACING?

HARD TRUTH: WHAT WORRIES ME THE MOST?

KIND RESPONSE: WHAT I ACTUALLY KNOW?

KIND RESPONSE: WHAT IS WITHIN MY CONTROL?

DATE: / /

Support Inventory

WHO OR WHAT HAS HELPED ME RECENTLY?

WHERE AM I CARRYING TOO MUCH ALONE?

ONE FORM OF SUPPORT I COULD ACCEPT OR SEEK?

DATE: / /

Financial & Life Stress

CURRENT FINANCIAL STRESSOR?

WHAT IS OUTSIDE OF MY CONTROL?

WHAT IS REALISTICALLY MANAGEABLE THIS WEEK?

ONE STABILISING STEP I CAN TAKE:

DATE: / /

Steadying Reflection

WHAT SMALL ACTION HELPED TODAY?

WHAT WILL I CONTINUE?

WHAT CAN I RELEASE FOR NOW?

WHAT FEELS MORE STABLE THAN BEFORE?

DATE: / /

Grounding Page

WHAT FEELS MOST URGENT RIGHT NOW?

WHAT CAN BE ADDRESSED TODAY WITHOUT OVERLOAD?

WHAT CAN SAFELY WAIT?

ONE SMALL ACTION TO REGAIN CLARITY:

DATE: / /

Capacity Check!

HOW MUCH ENERGY DO I REALISTICALLY HAVE TODAY?

WHERE AM I OVEREXTENDING?

WHAT CAN BE SIMPLIFIED, POSTPONED, OR DROPPED?

ONE ADJUSTMENT TO MAKE TODAY MANAGEABLE:

DATE: / /

Hard Truth/Kind Response

HARD TRUTH: THE REALITY I AM FACING?

HARD TRUTH: WHAT WORRIES ME THE MOST?

KIND RESPONSE: WHAT I ACTUALLY KNOW?

KIND RESPONSE: WHAT IS WITHIN MY CONTROL?

DATE: / /

Support Inventory

WHO OR WHAT HAS HELPED ME RECENTLY?

WHERE AM I CARRYING TOO MUCH ALONE?

ONE FORM OF SUPPORT I COULD ACCEPT OR SEEK?

DATE: / /

Financial & Life Stress

CURRENT FINANCIAL STRESSOR?

WHAT IS OUTSIDE OF MY CONTROL?

WHAT IS REALISTICALLY MANAGEABLE THIS WEEK?

ONE STABILISING STEP I CAN TAKE:

DATE: / /

Steadying Reflection

WHAT SMALL ACTION HELPED TODAY?

WHAT WILL I CONTINUE?

WHAT CAN I RELEASE FOR NOW?

WHAT FEELS MORE STABLE THAN BEFORE?

DATE: / /

Grounding Page

WHAT FEELS MOST URGENT RIGHT NOW?

WHAT CAN BE ADDRESSED TODAY WITHOUT OVERLOAD?

WHAT CAN SAFELY WAIT?

ONE SMALL ACTION TO REGAIN CLARITY:

DATE: / /

Capacity Check!

HOW MUCH ENERGY DO I REALISTICALLY HAVE TODAY?

WHERE AM I OVEREXTENDING?

WHAT CAN BE SIMPLIFIED, POSTPONED, OR DROPPED?

ONE ADJUSTMENT TO MAKE TODAY MANAGEABLE:

DATE: / /

Hard Truth/Kind Response

HARD TRUTH: THE REALITY I AM FACING?

HARD TRUTH: WHAT WORRIES ME THE MOST?

KIND RESPONSE: WHAT I ACTUALLY KNOW?

KIND RESPONSE: WHAT IS WITHIN MY CONTROL?

DATE: / /

Support Inventory

WHO OR WHAT HAS HELPED ME RECENTLY?

WHERE AM I CARRYING TOO MUCH ALONE?

ONE FORM OF SUPPORT I COULD ACCEPT OR SEEK?

DATE: / /

Financial & Life Stress

CURRENT FINANCIAL STRESSOR?

WHAT IS OUTSIDE OF MY CONTROL?

WHAT IS REALISTICALLY MANAGEABLE THIS WEEK?

ONE STABILISING STEP I CAN TAKE:

DATE: / /

Steadying Reflection

WHAT SMALL ACTION HELPED TODAY?

WHAT WILL I CONTINUE?

WHAT CAN I RELEASE FOR NOW?

WHAT FEELS MORE STABLE THAN BEFORE?

DATE: / /

Grounding Page

WHAT FEELS MOST URGENT RIGHT NOW?

WHAT CAN BE ADDRESSED TODAY WITHOUT OVERLOAD?

WHAT CAN SAFELY WAIT?

ONE SMALL ACTION TO REGAIN CLARITY:

DATE: / /

Capacity Check!

HOW MUCH ENERGY DO I REALISTICALLY HAVE TODAY?

WHERE AM I OVEREXTENDING?

WHAT CAN BE SIMPLIFIED, POSTPONED, OR DROPPED?

ONE ADJUSTMENT TO MAKE TODAY MANAGEABLE:

DATE: / /

Hard Truth/Kind Response

HARD TRUTH: THE REALITY I AM FACING?

HARD TRUTH: WHAT WORRIES ME THE MOST?

KIND RESPONSE: WHAT I ACTUALLY KNOW?

KIND RESPONSE: WHAT IS WITHIN MY CONTROL?

DATE: / /

Support Inventory

WHO OR WHAT HAS HELPED ME RECENTLY?

WHERE AM I CARRYING TOO MUCH ALONE?

ONE FORM OF SUPPORT I COULD ACCEPT OR SEEK?

DATE: / /

Financial & Life Stress

CURRENT FINANCIAL STRESSOR?

WHAT IS OUTSIDE OF MY CONTROL?

WHAT IS REALISTICALLY MANAGEABLE THIS WEEK?

ONE STABILISING STEP I CAN TAKE:

DATE: / /

Steadying Reflection

WHAT SMALL ACTION HELPED TODAY?

WHAT WILL I CONTINUE?

WHAT CAN I RELEASE FOR NOW?

WHAT FEELS MORE STABLE THAN BEFORE?

DATE: / /

Grounding Page

WHAT FEELS MOST URGENT RIGHT NOW?

WHAT CAN BE ADDRESSED TODAY WITHOUT OVERLOAD?

WHAT CAN SAFELY WAIT?

ONE SMALL ACTION TO REGAIN CLARITY:

DATE: / /

Capacity Check!

HOW MUCH ENERGY DO I REALISTICALLY HAVE TODAY?

WHERE AM I OVEREXTENDING?

WHAT CAN BE SIMPLIFIED, POSTPONED, OR DROPPED?

ONE ADJUSTMENT TO MAKE TODAY MANAGEABLE:

DATE: / /

Hard Truth/Kind Response

HARD TRUTH: THE REALITY I AM FACING?

HARD TRUTH: WHAT WORRIES ME THE MOST?

KIND RESPONSE: WHAT I ACTUALLY KNOW?

KIND RESPONSE: WHAT IS WITHIN MY CONTROL?

DATE: / /

Support Inventory

WHO OR WHAT HAS HELPED ME RECENTLY?

WHERE AM I CARRYING TOO MUCH ALONE?

ONE FORM OF SUPPORT I COULD ACCEPT OR SEEK?

DATE: / /

Financial & Life Stress

CURRENT FINANCIAL STRESSOR?

WHAT IS OUTSIDE OF MY CONTROL?

WHAT IS REALISTICALLY MANAGEABLE THIS WEEK?

ONE STABILISING STEP I CAN TAKE:

DATE: / /

Steadying Reflection

WHAT SMALL ACTION HELPED TODAY?

WHAT WILL I CONTINUE?

WHAT CAN I RELEASE FOR NOW?

WHAT FEELS MORE STABLE THAN BEFORE?

DATE: / /

Grounding Page

WHAT FEELS MOST URGENT RIGHT NOW?

WHAT CAN BE ADDRESSED TODAY WITHOUT OVERLOAD?

WHAT CAN SAFELY WAIT?

ONE SMALL ACTION TO REGAIN CLARITY:

DATE: / /

Capacity Check!

HOW MUCH ENERGY DO I REALISTICALLY HAVE TODAY?

WHERE AM I OVEREXTENDING?

WHAT CAN BE SIMPLIFIED, POSTPONED, OR DROPPED?

ONE ADJUSTMENT TO MAKE TODAY MANAGEABLE:

DATE: / /

Hard Truth/Kind Response

HARD TRUTH: THE REALITY I AM FACING?

HARD TRUTH: WHAT WORRIES ME THE MOST?

KIND RESPONSE: WHAT I ACTUALLY KNOW?

KIND RESPONSE: WHAT IS WITHIN MY CONTROL?

DATE: / /

Support Inventory

WHO OR WHAT HAS HELPED ME RECENTLY?

WHERE AM I CARRYING TOO MUCH ALONE?

ONE FORM OF SUPPORT I COULD ACCEPT OR SEEK?

DATE: / /

Financial & Life Stress

CURRENT FINANCIAL STRESSOR?

WHAT IS OUTSIDE OF MY CONTROL?

WHAT IS REALISTICALLY MANAGEABLE THIS WEEK?

ONE STABILISING STEP I CAN TAKE:

DATE: / /

Steadying Reflection

WHAT SMALL ACTION HELPED TODAY?

WHAT WILL I CONTINUE?

WHAT CAN I RELEASE FOR NOW?

WHAT FEELS MORE STABLE THAN BEFORE?

DATE: / /

Grounding Page

WHAT FEELS MOST URGENT RIGHT NOW?

WHAT CAN BE ADDRESSED TODAY WITHOUT OVERLOAD?

WHAT CAN SAFELY WAIT?

ONE SMALL ACTION TO REGAIN CLARITY:

DATE: / /

Capacity Check!

HOW MUCH ENERGY DO I REALISTICALLY HAVE TODAY?

WHERE AM I OVEREXTENDING?

WHAT CAN BE SIMPLIFIED, POSTPONED, OR DROPPED?

ONE ADJUSTMENT TO MAKE TODAY MANAGEABLE:

DATE: / /

Hard Truth/Kind Response

HARD TRUTH: THE REALITY I AM FACING?

HARD TRUTH: WHAT WORRIES ME THE MOST?

KIND RESPONSE: WHAT I ACTUALLY KNOW?

KIND RESPONSE: WHAT IS WITHIN MY CONTROL?

DATE: / /

Support Inventory

WHO OR WHAT HAS HELPED ME RECENTLY?

WHERE AM I CARRYING TOO MUCH ALONE?

ONE FORM OF SUPPORT I COULD ACCEPT OR SEEK?

DATE: / /

Financial & Life Stress

CURRENT FINANCIAL STRESSOR?

WHAT IS OUTSIDE OF MY CONTROL?

WHAT IS REALISTICALLY MANAGEABLE THIS WEEK?

ONE STABILISING STEP I CAN TAKE:

DATE: / /

Steadying Reflection

WHAT SMALL ACTION HELPED TODAY?

WHAT WILL I CONTINUE?

WHAT CAN I RELEASE FOR NOW?

WHAT FEELS MORE STABLE THAN BEFORE?

Notes

Did this journal help you?

Consider passing it on to someone who might need it.

Available on Amazon

The Steady Day Journal

Spence & Co.

Made in the USA
Monee, IL
08 November 2026

67968589R00095